How to Respond

Satanism

Revised Edition

Bruce G. Frederickson

This series was initiated to meet a need expressed by the members of The Lutheran Church—Missouri Synod in convention in 1975. The books were developed first under the umbrella of the Synod's Board for Evangelism, now part of the Board for Congregational Services.

Scripture quotations are taken from THE HOLY BIBLE, NEW INTERNATIONAL VERSION®. Copyright © 1973, 1978, 1984 by the International Bible Society. Used by permission of Zondervan Publishing House. All rights reserved.

The "NIV" and "New International Version" trademarks are registered in the United States Patent and Trademark Office by the International Bible Society. Use of either trademark requires the permission of the International Bible Society.

Originally published as *How to Respond to Satanism* in The Response Series, © 1988 Concordia Publishing House.

Copyright © 1988, 1995 Concordia Publishing House
3558 S. Jefferson Avenue, St. Louis, MO 63118-3968
Manufactured in the United States of America

Revised edition 1995

Library of Congress Cataloging-in-Publication Data

Federickson, Bruce G., 1946–
    Satanism / Bruce G. Frederickson.
        p.   cm.   — (How to respond series)
    Rev. ed. of: How to respond to—Satanism. © 1988.
    Includes bibliographical references.
    ISBN 0-570-04678-5
    1. Satanism—Controversial literature. 2. Devil. I. Title. II. Series.
BL480.F73   1995
261.2'1—dc20   95-8597

1 2 3 4 5 6 7 8 9 10   04 03 02 01 00 99 98 97 96 95

The Author

Bruce Frederickson has researched, studied, and spoken extensively on the subjects of cults, the occult, and Satanism. This path began 22 years ago when, as a parish pastor in Iowa, he encountered people who had had contact in these areas. This was especially true with the young people he later worked with while chaplain and chair of the religion department of Concordia Academy Lutheran High School in St. Paul, Minn.

Pastor Frederickson has followed the rapid development of Satanism books, magazines, and news and has developed an extensive library of material on Satanism and the occult. He has spoken to church groups and pastors' conferences and has led seminars on the topics of the cults, the occult, Satanism, and the New Age Movement. He often has counseled people who are troubled by involvement in the occult, as well as their families and friends. Pastor Frederickson presently serves as senior pastor of Messiah Lutheran Church, Mounds View, Minn.

As a topic, Satanism may easily be either sensationalized or ignored. Between these extremes, Frederickson offers a realistic and biblical Christian approach to the occult and Satanism. He clearly outlines the dangers of both from a biblical perspective. He also provides suggestions for a positive Christian response to these temptations and for Christian spiritual warfare and victorious living.

Contents

1

Introduction: Satan Is Real!

In spite of the crowds and noise, contestants in a run must focus on the goal, the finish line. Christians must too, for they are participants in the most important race: the race of life. St. Paul describes some of the difficulties of this race as he characterizes the followers of this world:

A mother was afraid because her children were home alone when a severe weather alert announced that a tornado was sighted near their home. She drove home rapidly through a torrential rainstorm only to find her children calmly watching television. "Didn't you see the warnings? Why didn't you take cover?" They calmly replied, "We were watching a video, Mom. We didn't know there was any danger." We, however, have no such excuse. We know the signs of the times and that the end is fast approaching.

> But mark this: There will be terrible times in the last days. People will be lovers of themselves, lovers of money, boastful, proud, abusive, disobedient to their parents, ungrateful, unholy, without love, unforgiving, slanderous, without self-control, brutal, not lovers of the good, treacherous, rash, conceited, lovers of pleasure rather than lovers of God—having a form of godliness but denying its power. Have nothing to do with them (2 Timothy 3:1–5).

In this book you will learn more about the devil, where he came from, and how he affects you. You will learn what Scripture says about Satan and, more importantly, you will learn about God Himself. You will learn to avoid dangerous practices and to challenge things that others may consider harmless.

The end is near!

The Reality of Satan

Do you believe in a real devil as described in the Bible? Some think that the devil is just a leftover remnant from the Middle Ages. Others believe he is a myth, that he doesn't really exist. What do *you* believe?

There is a power that moves in our world today. Evidences of evil, present throughout history and now liberally sprinkled throughout the daily paper must either be dismissed or accepted as real. Some people ask, "Where does such evil come from? Why do such terrible things happen? How can people be so mean?" The answer is plain. These accounts of evil—along with the testimony of the Bible—leave little doubt that the devil is real. The presence of evil illustrates that Satan is very active in this world, trying to gain a foothold in people's lives (Ephesians 4:27).

Satan is first mentioned in the third chapter of the Bible as a creature who tempts people to disobey God. In the third-last chapter of the Bible, Satan's defeat is announced. He is sent to darkness and despair where he belongs. His time is short. Although defeated, Satan frantically tries with his dying gasps to lead people away from God. The closer you get to Jesus, the harder and faster Satan works on you. Of course, not everyone reads the Bible, and those who do don't always believe what it says. Yet the end of all things will overtake

Even if you can't see spiritual dangers, they still are real. One of Satan's most powerful tricks is his cloak of invisibility. But you, soldier of Christ, are armed with the Word of God. Nothing is stronger!

8

everyone just the same. As Judgment Day approaches, you can count on Satan to work even harder to drag you away from your Savior.

Battling the Unseen

As a way to help her students learn to be wary of the unseen, a teacher once told her students that she was going out into the hallway and would close the door behind her. She warned the students that no matter what happened, they were not to open the door or peek out. She then made a commotion in the hallway. When they could stand it no more, the students carefully turned the knob and opened it just a crack. Suddenly the teacher grabbed one student's wrist and jerked him out into the hallway, frightening him significantly. While we may disagree with that tactic, her point was valid: curiosity about the unknown can lead us through all kinds of doorways into strange and dangerous realities.

Like children who don't hear a weather warning or who don't heed one they do know about, not everyone knows or cares about the reality of this spiritual warfare. St. Paul, however, reminds us of its seriousness: "Our struggle is not against flesh and blood, but against the rulers, against the authorities, against the powers of this dark world and against the spiritual forces of evil in the heavenly realms" (Ephesians 6:12).

Satan's name means "adversary." Before a game, athletes often study films of their adversaries to discover flaws or mistakes that can be used to their advantage. Similarly, Christians can use the Bible to learn of Satan's trickery and craftiness and to become skilled at resisting him.

Each of us is like a chain. No matter how strong, everyone has at least one weak link. Satan tries to use the weakness of that link to destroy people who are precious to God. His methods vary. Evil spirits trouble and possess people (Matthew 8:28). With trickery and deceit Satan seeks to snatch the seed of God's Word from people's hearts (Matthew 13:19). He was so bold as to even tempt the Son of God (Matthew 4:1).

However, don't miss the victory of Jesus. Signs of the power of God and of His Anointed also fill every page of Scripture and are all around us. This is a battle in that the final results are already in. The Father gave His Son a "name that is above every name" (Philippians 2:9): the name "Jesus," which means "the Lord saves." He did save; Christ has won!

Satan does have one advantage: he has more experience in tempting than we have in resisting him. One the other hand, we have the advantage of Jesus at our side. Satan knows and fears Him. Jesus has already met Satan in deadly conflict and won—for us! Even the gates of hell shall never be successful against Christ and you, His followers (Matthew 16:18).

Signs of the End

In speaking about the end of all things, Jesus said, "Now learn this lesson from the fig tree: As soon as its twigs get tender and its leaves come out, you know that summer is near. Even so, when you see all these things, you know that it is near, right at the door" (Matthew 24:32–33). Jesus expects us to read the signs of the times and prepare for His glorious return. But remember: Satan also reads these signs—and he is frantic, for he doesn't know the exact time of Jesus' return.

In his haste, Satan leaves tracks—signs that he has been here. In history and the daily paper we find numerous accounts of evil and terrible events. Some think that Satan's activity in the world is intensifying. Actually we need not look for spectacular signs. We see simple signs such as false Christs (Matthew 24:5), conflict within families and between nations (Matthew 24:6; Mark 13:12), and people's love growing cold (Matthew 24:12).

Not too long ago, space travel, video screens, and instantaneous communication were fantasy and fiction. So also, a satanic church was once unthinkable. The words *satanic* and *church* seemed about as far apart as could be. But today there are churches that worship just about anyone or anything, including the devil.

In 1966, many were skeptical when Anton Szandor LaVey founded his First Church of Satan. When his *The Satanic Bible* outsold the real Bible on college campuses, spiritual leaders inquired. Parents and teachers expressed concerned about bizarre behavior of children. Law enforcement officials investigated strange evidence at crime scenes. Violent crime, especially among young people, has been increasingly linked to LaVey's *The Satanic Bible*. These influences pose an alarming threat to Christian faith and the life of God's people.

> This book will not convince you that the devil is real. However, perhaps it will help you accept the reality of evil in the world today and respond positively as a Christian. "Your enemy the devil prowls around like a roaring lion looking for someone to devour. Resist him, standing firm in the faith" (1 Peter 5:8–9).

We might wonder also about the increase of interest in the occult. *Occult* (which means "hidden") includes such things as fortune-telling, magick, and spiritism (communication with dead people). Once thought to be fantasy, many now accept the results of occult practices as real. People attempt to control others by magical powers. In attempting to communicate with the dead, some are like children who are unaware of storm warnings. They don't know and therefore don't believe that the devil is real or dangerous.

One of the most curious challenges to Christianity

comes from the very document that guarantees and protects religious freedom: the United States Constitution. Some Christians favor the quick passage of laws to outlaw groups they consider dangerous. They forget that at various times in history the Christian faith was endangered and followers of Jesus were legally persecuted, killed, and their organizations banned. As long as satanic groups do not interfere with constitutional freedoms, Christians find themselves in the awkward position of defending their civic right to exist. Although we do not agree with their beliefs, we recognize their First Amendment freedoms.

St. Paul writes, "The Spirit clearly says that in later times some will abandon the faith and follow deceiving spirits and things taught by demons" (1 Timothy 4:1). In his *Screwtape Letters*, C. S. Lewis says, "There are two equal and opposite errors into which our race can fall about the devils. One is to disbelieve their existence. The other is to believe, and to feel an excessive and unhealthy interest in them" (p. 3). Another Christian author wisely concludes that "one cannot just pick up the dark bolts of magical fire and drop them at will without getting burned" (F. W. Thomas, *Kingdom of Darkness;* quoted in Clifford Wilson and John Weldon, *Occult Shock and Psychic Forces*, pp. 13–14).

As previously mentioned, we have been warned of the terrible times that lie ahead (2 Timothy 3:1). Read the signs of the times, and know the end is fast approaching. Satan works hardest when he recognizes the last and greatest of the signs of Christ's return: the spread of the Gospel. "And this gospel of the kingdom will be preached in the whole world as a testimony to all nations, and then the end will come" (Matthew 24:14).

Studying Satanism is a lot like wading into the water. You may choose only to wet your feet, but you seldom do. You like what you feel, so you wade in deeper and deeper.

As you examine Satanism, use great caution lest Satan confuse and trap you. The information in this book is meant to familiarize you with the game plan of the enemy. Elusive as he is, you must never let down your guard.

Along with that caution, remember also that Jesus holds you closely and will never let you go (John 10:28). He protects you from "all the flaming arrows of the evil one" (Ephesians 6:16). When, in the Lord's Prayer, you pray "Deliver us from evil," you ask God to build a protective barrier between yourself and "the evil one," Satan; you ask for God's deliverance by Christ. Now, through faith in Him, you have it. Live in His victory!

2

The Enemy and His Footprints

Some people think Satan is everywhere and can do anything. That's what he would like everyone to believe, but we know from the Bible that he is merely the great pretender. He acts like God, but he is not God; he is powerful, but Christ is stronger. If Satan were stronger than God, how could Jesus just walk away from him?

Jesus described Satan as a strong man who could be bound and whose house could be plundered (Matthew 12:29). Throughout His earthly ministry, Jesus proceeded to plunder Satan's kingdom and diminish his power. And on the cross and by His resurrection victory, Christ defeated Satan.

Why, then, does Scripture make such a big deal about him? I suggest two reasons. First, Satan is not dead or even weakened to the point of death. Although the ultimate victory still belongs to God, Satan is strong enough to win far too many of the daily battles for our souls—and we are too weak by ourselves to defend against him. Second, I believe the Bible repeatedly warns against Satan because of his most important disguise: invisibility. How can mere humans defend against the invisible? "Our struggle is not against flesh and blood, but ... against the spiritual forces of evil in the heavenly realms" (Ephesians 6:12).

In spite of his cloak of invisibility, Satan cannot cover

his tracks. As mentioned in chapter 1, Satan's evil work can be traced throughout history and in present-day news reports. Authorities now take seriously repeated accounts of devil worship, mutilation, killings, and sinister sacrifices. To doubt that Satan continues to be active in our world today is to doubt a rising mountain of evidence.

Who Is Satan and Where Did He Come From?

The Bible doesn't describe Satan's origin in great detail. The "ancient serpent" is identified as "the devil, or Satan" (Revelation 12:9). Scripture speaks of angels who sinned (2 Peter 2:4) and "angels who did not keep their positions of authority but abandoned their own home" (Jude 6). When this initial rebellion of the devil and his evil angels took place the Bible does not say. But ever since Satan and his demons rebelled, this evil being seeks to discredit God and harm His people. Job 1–2 describes the devil as a being who roams the earth and seeks to afflict God's servants. This he has done from the very beginning of the world. Already in Eden, Satan tempted Adam and Eve to join him in the desire to be like God (Genesis 3).

The Bible uses many names to identify or describe this enemy of God and His people, but *devil* and *Satan* are the most frequently used terms. *Devil* (Matthew 4:1), which means "accuser" or "slanderer," tells us how he does his work. He accused God's first human creatures in the garden. He accused Job. *Satan* means "opponent" or "adversary." He is not for us; he is against us and God.

Tempter is another name for the devil, which also describes how he works. He tries to deceptively lead people away from God and His goodness.

Jesus called the devil *the father of lies,* for he has been a "liar" and "a murderer from the beginning" (John 8:44).

We can never know truth from the devil, because he even turns the truth into a lie.

In teaching His disciples to pray, Jesus asked the Father to "deliver us from evil." This could also be translated as "deliver us from *the evil one,*" that is, Satan.

Satan doesn't work alone. He commands countless other invisible spirits (Mark 5:9). Together, they work for the spiritual destruction of Christ, His people, and His church.

The Bible has much to say about the soul-destroying activities of Satan. Study, for example, Luke 22:31; John 13:2; 1 Corinthians 10:20–21; 2 Corinthians 4:4; Ephesians 2:2; and 1 Timothy 4:1. Satan is powerful and evil. Remember, though, God is stronger (1 John 4:4).

Tracking the Enemy

By studying its tracks, a hunter can identify his prey before he actually sees it. We wish that identifying Satan and his work were always that easy. However, his presence is obvious in at least three major areas of occult interest: *fortune-telling, magick,* and *spiritism.*

Fortune-telling, a broad category, includes all attempts to know the future through means such as tarot cards, psychic predictions, and other divination devices. This occult practice is based on a belief that these artificial devices allow people to gain information about the future or other people and to use it to their own advantage.

Those who practice *occult magic* prefer to spell the word "magick" in order to distinguish it from sleight-of-hand magic such as pulling a rabbit out of a hat. Those who practice occult magick claim to be able to manipulate people and objects by using a power outside themselves. Since God's power would not be available for such a practice, the only other source of such power is Satan.

Spiritism is based on the belief that people can contact

17

the spirits of dead persons. Such contact is usually established by persons called "mediums." This is always done at the expense of other persons in order to gain control over them. *Spiritualism,* the so-called "Christian" side of spiritism, differs only in that it uses Christian terminology. In reality, spiritualism is only a poorly disguised attempt to whitewash something that is still evil and forbidden by God.

Another area of satanic influence, the New Age Movement, is described in another book in this How to Respond series, *The New Age Movement.* This book details how false and dangerous beliefs about spirituality can lead to a false sense of security, which in turn can cause many Christians to abandon their faith in Christ and build their lives upon the sinking sand of Satan's schemes.

As people become more deeply involved in the occult and New Age practices, some widen their interests. They become more deeply involved with the devil and his evil spirits. Some actually worship the devil or Satan. This is called *Satanism.* Christians, who go to church and worship God, may find it hard to imagine there are people who actually worship the devil. It seems so unreal that, when the First Church of Satan was founded in 1966, many Christians dismissed Satanism as foolish and harmless. But when evidence of Satanism began to appear throughout the country, Christians began to take a serious second look at the influences of Satan on our world and culture.

In his book *Turmoil in the Toybox* (pp. 174–75), author Phil Phillips neatly catalogs "forbidden practices" that God clearly condemns. The following are some:

1. *Enchantments*—influencing by charms and magical arts (Leviticus 19:26; Deuteronomy 18:10–12);
2. *Witchcraft/sorcery/magick/wizardry*—dealing with evil spirits through sorcery or magick (Deuteronomy 18:10–12; 2 Chronicles 33:6)

3. *Divination/soothsaying*—fortune-telling (Deuteronomy 18:10–14; Acts 16:16–24)
4. *Necromancy*—communicating with the dead through evil spirits (Deuteronomy 18:11; 1 Chronicles 10:13–14);
5. *Charm*—putting a spell on someone (Deuteronomy 18:11; Isaiah 19:3)
6. *Star Gazing/astrology*—suggestion that the stars control human affairs and character (Isaiah 47:12–15; Jeremiah 10:2)

All of these occult practices are clearly condemned by God throughout Scripture. We must constantly guard against the sinister temptations to power and glory that Satan offers.

Satan Is a Defeated Enemy

Satanism is a very real force that must be confronted. Do not, however, become afraid and, like the ostrich, put your head in the sand. In doing so you only provide a target for the devil. Until Christ returns, Satan will continue to scheme and plan ways to lead people away from Christ. Yet Scripture clearly reveals the victory of God's Son, Jesus, and the abundant life that God offers to all who receive His love and follow Him.

This book provides information to help you identify Satan and his influences. Since Satan attacked our first parents, Adam and Eve, and even went to battle with the Son of God, he will not think twice about attacking any human. You must always be on your guard against the influence of evil in our world.

Since by His death on the cross Jesus defeated Satan, some ask how Satan can still "prowl around" and tempt people. A young boy was watching his grandfather kill chickens. He noticed that when their heads were chopped off, they remained active for a short time. One even ran down the road a few feet. "Why, he must still be alive," said the boy. "No," the old man replied, "he just thinks he is."

Why All the Interest?

Why is there so much interest in the occult, the New Age, and Satanism? These subjects were not publicized much during the first three-quarters of this century. Why now? There are a number of reasons.

Power: Use of the occult and Satanism offers power and control to people who otherwise may feel powerless. Some who have left Satanism testify that the lure of power was the great draw.

Understanding/knowledge: Others participated in Satanism in an attempt to explain the unexplainable. We live in a time when, in spite of science, much remains unexplained, especially supernatural events. The occult helps some people believe what they can't see.

Curiosity: Some people are just plain curious—and become hooked when it "works." "Why not see if the Ouija board works for me? Could my horoscope help me even one day a week? What's so bad about taking just a peek?"

Whatever the reason, we need to heed Paul's warning: "I am afraid that just as Eve was deceived by the serpent's cunning, your minds may somehow be led astray from your sincere and pure

We are living in the last times. "Dear children, this is the last hour; and as you have heard that the antichrist is coming, even now many antichrists have come" (1 John 2:18). "For the time will come when men will not put up with sound doctrine. Instead, to suit their own desires, they will gather around them a great number of teachers to say what their itching ears want to hear" (2 Timothy 4:3).

devotion to Christ" (2 Corinthians 11:3). Paul encourages us to be on our guard "in order that Satan might not outwit us. For we are not unaware of his schemes" (2 Corinthians 2:11). If you gain nothing else from your study, learn to *beware* and to *be aware*.

Thanks Be to God Who Gives Us the Victory!

All who bear Christ's name must clearly proclaim that He is King of kings and Lord of lords. As God's children, we never lose sight of the victory that Christ won for us on the cross. We savor His death for us and cherish His resurrection as proof that we, too, shall live forever. We no longer need to live in the fear, darkness, and doubt that Satan offers. Instead, we can learn to live confidently in the love, light, and certainty that God offers all who believe and trust in Jesus. As long as Satan can roam the earth, he will remain a threat to followers of Christ. Still, we know that Christ too is alive. He who has given you life will also give you an abundant and eternal life with Him forever. "My sheep listen to My voice; I know them, and they follow Me. I give them eternal life, and they shall never perish; no one can snatch them out of My hand" (John 10:27–28).

3

The Whispers of God

God Speaks

God usually doesn't shout to get the attention of His people. Often He speaks in a "gentle whisper" (1 Kings 19:12). Some listen when God speaks; others ignore His voice.

Satan too speaks; he has no intention of remaining silent. Satan sometimes rears his ugly head and speaks directly to people. Sometimes he speaks through his demon foot soldiers. But whether he speaks directly or through others, those who listen and follow are destined for sadness, horror, and confusion.

When our first parents were placed in Paradise, God restricted them from only one tree. On one fateful day, Satan tempted Eve; she ate from the tree, then she shared with her husband, and he also ate willingly. It seemed that Satan had won. He had tempted God's first two human beings to doubt God's Word and turn away from Him. God had every right to throw them out; instead He spoke words. He said to Satan, but Adam and Eve no doubt overheard: "I will put enmity between you and the woman, and between your offspring and hers" (Genesis 3:15a). God condemned Satan. "He will crush your head," and in the process, "you will strike His heel" (Genesis 3:15b).

God was able to look down through history to another incident, years later. In fulfillment of His promise, our heavenly Father agreed that His own Son should be wounded for our sake. He saw His Son give His life into death on a cross and, by the shedding of His blood, crush and defeat Satan. The Father heard the words, "It is finished" (John 19:30).

Satan knew he could never defeat God, so he continued to attack God's people. Ever since that time, Satan has been actively "looking for someone to devour" (1 Peter 5:8). That's why we continually need to remember God's promise: "He [Jesus] will crush your [Satan's] head" (Genesis 3:15b). Satan knows it and so do we!

Move through history to the book of Job. Do you marvel that God allowed Satan to be on the loose? God asked, "Where have you come from" (Job 1:7)? God had not lost track of Satan; He knew exactly where Satan had been. And the plot the devil hatched against God and Job came to naught.

Satan is always subject to God. So why does he keep fighting a war he knows he can't win? Satan has nothing to lose and everything to gain in the individual battles. If anyone will follow his crafty ways, Satan scores another victory. But when Satan's ways are exposed and the light of Jesus' love is emphasized, God scores an even greater victory.

Satan's boldest attack was on God's Son, Jesus Christ (Matthew 4:1–11). If Satan could trick Jesus into "proving" that He was God's Son instead of trusting the Father's words, then Satan would win. But why would Satan use such foolish things as bread, jumping from a high place, or bowing before him as temp-

Martin Luther said, "Satan is always *God's devil.*" Although Satan is always on the prowl, he is always under God's jurisdiction. Still, the moment we give Satan an inch, he takes a mile. Be on your guard lest Satan catch you unawares! "Resist the devil, and he will [must] flee from you" (James 4:7)!

tations for Jesus? They don't look very difficult. Consider Satan's plight. Although the battle in the Garden of Eden had been a mixture of temporary victory and defeat for Satan, here comes God's Son for the ultimate showdown. Satan was terrified! If he could just divert Jesus' trust in the Father and His plan, then Jesus wouldn't be any better off than Satan himself. "If ... if ... if ...," Satan challenged. Each time Jesus replied, "It is written ..." Although He possessed the greatest power imaginable, Jesus used only that which is also available to us: God's Word. For us, though, the sweetest words in the entire account come at the end: "Then the devil left Him, and angels came and attended Him" (v. 11). Although Satan was bold enough to attack Jesus, he didn't win. Nor could he ever!

Why did God allow His Son to be in such a position? So that Jesus might be fully human as well as fully God, and, thus, take our place under the Law and its condemnation.

We assume that anyone who knows about Satan and what he stands for will immediately turn around and run in the opposite direction, using God's Word as Jesus did. Sadly, many listen to Satan's voice and obey. They follow the devil and are drawn into his evil web. Occult fortune-telling and magick may seem harmless. Those who practice spiritism or are involved in the New Age Movement may appear to only be caught up in a passing fad. But like a spider, Satan spins a very sticky web of intrigue, appeal, and innocence that eventually leads deeper into Satanism.

Satan Goes Fishing

On the end of most fishing lines is a reverse hook called a barb. When Satan goes fishing for us, he doesn't let us see the barb; rather, he covers it with attractive bait.

As a master counterfeiter, Satan cleverly copies God's spiritual gifts as bait. For example, in biblical history God gave to some the gift of prophecy; occult powers claim the same ability to look into the future. God gave to some the ability to perform miracles; so does Satan. Note Jesus' comment on these feats: "Many will say to Me on that day, 'Lord, Lord, did we not prophesy in Your name, and in Your name drive out demons and perform many miracles?' Then I will tell them plainly, 'I never knew you. Away from Me, you evildoers' " (Matthew 7:22–23)!

No one is helped by Satan. Jesus said, "Not everyone who says to Me, 'Lord, Lord,' will enter the kingdom of heaven, but only he who does the will of My Father who is in heaven" (Matthew 7:21).

In spite of God's warning, some people nibble at the bait—harmlessly for a time, unaware they are going against their Creator. But they never know when Satan will jerk the line and set the hook.

Jesus compared people to sheep (John 10). His kingdom is like a pen in which the sheep are kept. Jesus, the shepherd, enters by the gate. The sheep hear His voice and follow Him, because they *know* Him. Thieves and robbers always enter by another way, often by climbing the fence.

When people claim supernatural, spiritual power not promised in the Bible, how do you test the spirits? How can you recognize Satan's deadly tricks? Jesus said, "The thief comes only to steal and kill and destroy; I have come that they may have life, and have it to the full" (John 10:10).

Look at things you can't explain with your five senses. "Are the lusts of only one individual or group being met, or are people really being helped and is God glorified? Do people involved in occult and satanic activities really receive an abundant life, or do they forfeit the only real life that they ever had?" Use the information in this book to answer those questions for yourself. Perhaps you will also help someone else answer similar questions.

What Do You Do Now?

From the beginning, sinners have blamed others—even God—for their problems (James 1:13–15). When confronted by God, Adam blamed the woman whom God put into the garden (Genesis 3:12). The theme of the book of Job and the rest of human history is not "Whose fault is it that Job is/I am having a bad day?" That is a satanic question. The devil tempts us to point the finger of blame for our problems at someone else. He wants to destroy every happy relationship with God.

In toying with forbidden practices, God's children shift their loyalty from God to Satan. All of the evil practices described in this book can lead to unrestrained worship of Satan. God doesn't hesitate to express His displeasure when His people turn away from Him. But He is *always* willing to welcome them back. If you have ever, even remotely, been involved in things like this, acknowledge it before God. Know that you are standing before your loving Father as you tell Him you are sorry and heartsick for having gone against His Word. He embraces you in His forgiving arms. In faith, accept His freedom and forgiveness and pray for protection from further influence by Satan and his evil spirits.

In his great hymn "A Mighty Fortress Is Our God," Martin Luther wrote, "Though devils all the world should fill, All eager to devour us, We tremble not, we fear no ill, They shall not overpow'r us. This world's prince may still Scowl fierce as he will, He can harm us none, He's judged; the deed is done; One little word can fell him." (*Lutheran Worship* 298)

Long ago during Passover, God's children marked their doors with the blood of a sacrificial lamb. You can claim the protection of the blood of *the* Lamb, Jesus Christ. "How much more, then, will the blood of Christ, who through the eternal Spirit offered Himself unblemished to God, cleanse our consciences from acts that lead to death, so that we may serve the living God" (Hebrews 9:14)!

Be Aware and Beware!

In our study of Satanism, we must exercise care. As evidence of Satanism has increased, misinterpreted evidence and sensational rumors have launched many misguided witch-hunts and frightened many Christians. Just because we don't understand something doesn't mean it is occult or satanic. God said, "Test the spirits to see whether they are from God" and confess "that Jesus Christ has come in the flesh" (1 John 4:1–2).

History has taught us to guard against unrestrained witch-hunts. Some people in colonial Massachusetts probably *were* practicing Satanism and dabbling in the occult. Others were judged guilty by association and executed. Some died simply because a nearby baby cried or some milk turned up sour as they passed by. Such activities warn us not to overreact against any negative influence. Test the spirits. Are God's Word and Christ's death and resurrection compromised? Are people helped or used?

Christ has promised to be with us always (Matthew 28:20). We need to repent daily of our sin and pledge ourselves to lead a life that glorifies our Savior, Jesus. He wants only the best for us. "I have come that they may have life, and have it to the full" (John 10:10).

In the next three chapters we will deal with the broad categories of Satanism. *Religious Satanists* are visible satanic groups with leaders, organizations, and buildings. Underground *satanic cults* often spring up as a result of the popular influence of the visible groups. So-called *self-styled Satanists* may be the most dangerous, since they form their own group modeled after a variety of sources.

4

Satan Visible: Religious Satanists

What Is Satanism?

As a religion and a belief system, Satanism goes beyond the occult. In its simplest and purest form, Satanism is the worship of and service to Satan, who demands to be worshiped (Matthew 4:9). But whenever people worship and serve the creature rather than the Creator, they turn away from God's forgiveness and peace. According to Romans 1:25, they are condemned because they exchange the truth of God for a lie of Satan.

Some people try to distinguish between the occult and Satanism. They claim that since practice of the occult existed before Christianity, it cannot be satanic. Nor, therefore, can practitioners of the occult in our modern era be satanic—so they claim. However, Satan was already seeking the allegiance of humanity in the Garden of Eden. His goal will never change: he wants to replace God.

Satanism in the Old Testament

The Old Testament clearly evidences the activity of Satan and his demons. The Canaanites, who lived in the Promised Land before the Israelites arrived, worshiped a god known as Baal. Their worship included animal sacrifice (Judges 6:25) and prostitution (Exodus 34:13). These two features of satanic worship have survived into modern times. Baal worshipers also mutilated themselves hoping to satisfy the wrath of their god (1 Kings 18:28).

When God's people arrived in the Promised Land, He directed them either to drive out or kill those who lived in the land (Deuteronomy 7:1–10). The idolatrous and occult practices of these people were an abomination to God. He did not want His people to copy their evil ways.

Although forbidden by God, spiritism and mediums who attempted to contact the dead survived (1 Samuel 28:8). In a desperate situation, even one of God's own leaders, King Saul, consulted a witch and was condemned for his faithlessness (1 Chronicles 10:13–14).

Satanism in the New Testament

We have already mentioned a most significant encounter between Satan and Christ (Matthew 4), but the New Testament contains many other accounts of occult and satanic activities. Philip converted a magick practitioner named Simon (Acts 8:9–24). Paul confronted a magician and false prophet (Acts 13:6–12) who opposed Paul's preaching about Christ. In Philippi, Paul and Silas met a slave girl whose masters made a lot of money because she could predict the future (Acts 16:16–18). When Paul drove an evil spirit from her, her fortune-telling abilities disappeared. In Ephesus, some occult practitioners repented and turned to God after hear-

Most Satanists trace their roots back to a ceremony called "The Black Mass." This is a mockery of the Roman Catholic main worship service. Satanists seek power by reversing Christian ceremonies and rituals. They may say the Lord's Prayer or one of the Christian creeds in reverse or pervert the Christian sacraments. All this is done to release the ultimate power they seek and to satisfy their every desire!

ing Paul preach (Acts 19:17–20). Devil worship also was a problem in at least three of the churches in Jesus' seven letters to Asia Minor (Revelation 2:9, 13; 3:9).

Missionaries today still may encounter occult and satanic activities similar to those described in the Bible. Such modern activities differ only in the mask worn by the practitioner and the tools by which the evil ends are reached. Sadly, many Christians today see no harm in the occult as long as they only "dabble" in it. God, however, condemns the occult, not because He wishes to spoil anyone's fun, but because the occult despises God and endangers even the dabblers. Occult activities open many dangerous doors for Satan to enter into the lives of unsuspecting Christians.

Satanism Since Bible Times

In A.D. 681, the Council of Toledo banned the so-called "Mass of the Dead," performed to secure someone's death. In 1231, the Roman Catholic Church established a court to detect and punish those guilty of forbidden teachings and ceremonies. They later identified and punished witches, diviners, and others who lived and taught contrary to God's Word.

An early reference to the Black Mass was in the trial of Lady Kyteler in Ireland in 1324. She was accused of practicing witchcraft, denying Christ, and defiling objects connected with Holy Communion. She also sacrificed animals and was accused of having intercourse with demon spirits. Other references to condemned satanic practices occurred in the Church of England in 1343, in Sweden in the 1600s, and in France during the reign of Louis XIV.

The Salem witch trials in the United States provide further evidence that Satanism has been around for awhile. These witch-hunts kept the idea of occult groups alive throughout most of the early history of this country.

Throughout the past several centuries, an alleged secret group called the Illumanati has supposedly been involved in occult and satanic activities in order to gain control of world affairs. Supposedly, only people with wealth and power are allowed to join.

The German dictator Adolph Hitler was heavily into the occult. At the Nürenberg trials, a witness confessed to terrible crimes, including the beheading of a victim as part of a human sacrifice and the use of body parts for a secret communion service of leaders. Hitler's suicide on April 30 may have been planned to coincide with one of the highest dates on the witches' calendar, Walpurgisnacht.

Modern Satanism

Modern Satanism can be traced to Aleister Crowley. Born in 1875 to a devout Christian family in England, he was introduced to occult ideas and techniques by an occultist named Eliphas Levi. Crowley rebelled against his strict Christian upbringing. He rejected Christ and sought supernatural guidance by joining an occult group called the Temple and the Hermetic Order of the Golden Dawn. Denied advancement in that group because of his homosexual tendencies, Crowley formed his own group, the Ordo Temple Orientis. Using biblical references to the devil, he called himself "the great beast" and "666." He later joined several other occult/magick-related organizations in order to gain further power and guidance. Crowley thrived on publicity. He actually invited attacks to build his popularity.

Aleister Crowley believed that Satan was more powerful than God, and he ridiculed Christ as impotent. He was confident that Satan would win a final conflict. He established a magick study center in Scotland where he hoped to contact a "super mind" that he felt controlled the universe. Unfortunately, he sought guidance from Satan rather than from God. Finally, in Egypt, he contacted a spirit he called the "Holy Guardian Angel."

Crowley brought his ideas and followers to the United States, where religious freedom provided fertile soil in which to plant his evil ideas. His rituals were often conducted under the influence of drugs. His denial of any and all morality allowed him to do anything he wished. Descriptions of his sexual and drug experiences prove he died trying almost anything. Crowley died in 1947 after sowing the seeds of modern Satanism.

An Englishman named Gerald Gardner was influenced by Crowley. Through his writings this self-proclaimed witch "crafted" the rituals of modern witchcraft founded upon the Mother Goddess. Those who follow in the tradition of Gardner think of themselves as practicing primarily a nature religion, worshiping the creation rather than the Creator.

Gardner, and later LaVey, popularized the image of Baphomet, the horned god, as a popular symbol of witchcraft and Satanism. It depicts the devil as a goat at the left hand in Christ's judgment scene (Matthew 25:31–33). With two points in the air, the inverted five-pointed star (pentagram) resembles that goat's head and has become another popular symbol of Satanism. Inscribed inside a circle these symbols often serve as the altar in satanic worship. They frequently are found as evidence at sites of suspected satanic activity.

Religious Satanist Groups

Some authors suggest there are more than 450 identifiable satanic groups in the United States alone. However, most of these groups have no official organization or headquarters and don't publish any information or statistics. Therefore, almost no reliable information can be given on them. We can say, though, that two views about Satan himself stand out. The one view considers him to be an actual being; the other does not. This latter group claims that the term *Satan* merely represents raw human desire to be freely exercised in contrast to the moderation and abstinence of "weak" Christianity.

Satanism is openly practiced today as a legal religion in the United States. The best known satanic group is Anton LaVey's Church of Satan. The group itself has shunned notoriety, but many connected with the group have started local congregations, or grottoes, throughout the world. Some sources claim a worldwide membership approaching 10,000 members.

The Church of Satan

Anton Szandor LaVey

Anton Szandor LaVey was born in 1930. During his high school years, he came to believe that the mighty, not the meek, would inherit the earth. And outside of school, he began to study about the occult. Bored with regular studies he dropped out of school and joined the circus, where he worked as a substitute animal trainer. Later, he joined a carnival and continued to study the occult. He came to believe that youth, vigor, and strength were to be worshiped, because those who grew old and weak were soon discarded.

As an organ player in the carnival, he was able to view human nature at its base level:

> I would see men lusting after half-naked girls dancing at the carnival, and on Sunday morning and when I was playing organ for tent-show evangelists at the other end of the carnival lot, I would see these same men sitting in the pews with their wives and children, asking God to forgive them and purge them of carnal desires. And

the next Saturday night they'd be back at the carnival or some other place of indulgence. I knew then that the Christian church thrives on hypocrisy, and that man's carnal nature will win out no matter how much it is purged or scourged by any white-light religion (*The Satanic Bible*, p. 14).

After turning 21, LaVey studied criminology and became a police photographer for a time, but returned to entertainment as an organ player in nightclubs and theaters. But all the while he kept studying the occult and accumulated a vast library of books about occult practices. LaVey came to believe that Satan was the force responsible for all human desires. He even began to teach others in weekly classes.

What is the Christian church?" asked LaVey. "Denial of the sinful flesh" was his answer. He, instead, dreamed of a satanic church that would recapture the minds of people and allow them to use their fleshly desires as a cause for celebration rather than struggle.

Students were attracted as much to LaVey as to the subject. Soon a "Magic Circle" evolved from this group.

Formation of the Church of Satan

In 1966, Anton LaVey shaved his head, declared the dawn of the satanic age, and founded the Church of Satan—with himself as its high priest. He developed rituals for special occasions such as satanic weddings and funerals. The most popular was a destruction ritual that enabled participants to curse their enemies and proclaim victory over them. "God is dead, and Satan lives" became a password for rituals in LaVey's church. The rituals continue in the local grottoes (congregations).

Many Christians view this group as the most dangerous of all. Yet in reality, it is probably less harmful than

Who deserves what? *Jesus* encouraged His followers to turn the other cheek. In his *The Satanic Bible*, Anton LaVey encourages people to seek revenge. If, as LaVey suggests, we are to be kind only to those who deserve it, who would be the last left standing? Christ is stronger than Satan. His love truly conquers all!

some underground groups. Perhaps its greatest harm is in the books it distributes. LaVey's *The Satanic Bible*, a bestseller, has been found at the scenes of crimes suspected of being perpetrated by satanic cults and self-styled Satanists. From the outside, the book appears harmless; but its teachings, if believed and followed, embody a threat to Christians and their faith in the crucified and risen Savior.

The Nine Satanic Statements of *The Satanic Bible*

The cornerstone of LaVey's beliefs are his "nine satanic statements" (*The Satanic Bible*, p. 25). They attract intellectuals from every walk of life.

1. Satan represents indulgence instead of abstinence.
2. Satan represents vital existence instead of spiritual pipe dreams.
3. Satan represents undefiled wisdom instead of hypocritical self-deceit.
4. Satan represents kindness to those who deserve it instead of love wasted on ingrates.
5. Satan represents vengeance instead of turning the other cheek.
6. Satan represents responsibility to the responsible instead of concern for psychic vampires.
7. Satan represents man as just another animal, sometimes better, more often worse than those that walk on all fours, who, because of his "divine spiritual and intellectual development," has become the most vicious animal of all.

8. Satan represents all of the so-called sins, as they all lead to physical, mental, or emotional gratification.
9. Satan has been the best friend the church has ever had, as he has kept it in business all these years.

LaVey did not intend to found a new religion as such. Although he established rituals, there is no literal *worship* of Satan, since Satan does not literally exist. LaVey merely organized humanity's ancient rebellion against God.

Other Satanic Groups

Another organized group is the Temple of Set. *Set* is the Egyptian name for Satan. The high priest of this group, Michael A. Aquino, broke from LaVey's satanic church. As a member of the U.S. Army Reserve, Aquino has been regularly promoted and has received top-secret security clearance. Since the Constitution guarantees freedom of religious expression, he is open about his beliefs. He claims that the Christian church is responsible for placing Satan in a bad light. Satan is not evil, and Satanists are good people.

When Aquino appeared on *The Oprah Winfrey Show* (February 17, 1988), someone in the audience asked, "If you believe in the devil, do you want to go to hell when you die?" Although he effectively dodged the question, Aquino made it clear that his belief about the devil and hell differs from the more literal interpretation of Christianity.

Resist the Devil

Imagine you were standing beside Jesus as Satan approached Him. "If you are the Son of God, tell these stones to become bread" (Matthew 4:3). Do you hear the evil and destructive nature of what Satan said? "Serve yourself," he said. "Forget everyone else. Do what *you* want." We face similar temptations daily. The devil, the world, and our own sinful flesh seek to pull us away from God into Satan's waiting arms.

How do you answer the devil? Do you flex your spiritual muscles, hoping to frighten him away? Do you wonder whether you really are a child of God?

Never forget: in your Baptism, God called you by name; you *are* His child. Through Word and Sacrament, He keeps His loving arms around you. Therefore, you are never alone. Jesus promised to be with you always.

So, how can you respond to Satan's temptations? Jesus answered Satan by saying, "It is written" (Matthew 4:4). Jesus quoted His own Word, the Bible. Why? Because God's Word is God's dynamite for salvation and the only effective weapon against Satan (Romans 1:16; Ephesians 6:17). Remember Luther's words: "One little word can fell him"? The living Word is Jesus Christ, God's Son, who is "with you always, to the very end of the age" (Matthew 28:20).

"[T]he one [Jesus] who is in you is greater than the one [Satan] who is in the world" (1 John 4:4). Satan and Satanism are real, but when the devil sees Jesus in you, he must flee! Jesus is stronger. He died to win God's victory over Satan and evil. Now He lives to empower you to live a victorious life in Him.

5

On the Margin of the Visible: Satanic Cults

Satanic Cults

What is a cult? According to the dictionary, the word can be used for any religious group. Usually, however, we use the word *cult* to refer to a religious group that has splintered from a mainline religion.

Satanic cults are offshoots of mainline groups mentioned in the last chapter. Seeds of groups founded by Crowley, LaVey, and others have germinated into many modern satanic cults (some local rather than nationwide). Although not listed in the phone book, they function openly and publicly because their basic worship activities are constitutionally protected.

These groups worship the devil and perform some rituals that Christians find merely strange and repulsive. However, evidence indicates that satanic cult activities also have included animal sacrifices, burglaries, arson, and grave desecration.

An ABC News presentation, *20/20,* which aired on May 16, 1985, listed six evidences of satanic activity: *fixation with death,* use of certain *satanic paraphernalia, kidnapping, sexual abuse, cannibalism,* and *cremation.* This also explains how clever people, working for a very clever devil, can so successfully cover their tracks!

Incidents of criminal cult activity seem scattered and unconnected, but they might not be. Therefore, law enforcement agencies pool their information in an effort to discover some pattern of satanic practice to aid in prosecuting illegal cult activity. Groups such as Cult Crime Impact Network in Idaho, Bothered about Dungeons and Dragons in Virginia, and Parents' Music Resource Center, also in Virginia, collect and distribute information to parents and police officials who are concerned about the criminal nature of cultic activity.

> News items that hint at satanic activity run from lives ruined through Satanism to simply dabbling in the occult. Are they isolated and unrelated? Since these cultic groups are not very visible, little is known about them. Their activities often go undetected until they become illegal and dangerous.

In a 1988 magazine article, Dr. Roland Summit, assistant professor of psychiatry and a physician at County Harbor—UCLA Medical Center, said, "Anyone—possibly up until maybe today—who gathers a bunch of people to talk seriously about the possibility that ritualistic [sexual] abuse is real, risks being trivialized." He led discussions with a task force investigating connections between Satanism and child sexual abuse. They concluded that the subject was "being talked away and bargained down so that we don't have to deal with terrible, sordid things" (*The Daily Breeze*, Los Angeles, March 1, 1988).

Summit had been a witness at a criminal trial in which attendants at a day care center in Bakersfield, Calif., were charged with criminal sexual abuse. Although evidence pointed to organized, ritualistic abuse, it was dismissed. Then Dr. Summit began to receive pleading phone calls from desperate people in widely separated locations throughout the U.S. Each came with identical stories of children being ritualistically abused. The incidents often had occurred at day care centers and involved individuals whose dress, symbols, and jewelry identified them with a religious community. Unfortunately, the children often lacked the necessary names, dates, and places. But as clues mounted, officials could no longer sweep the evidence under the carpet. Similar stories of ritualistic abuse with satanic overtones were far too frequent to be ignored. However, when people claim evidence of criminal satanic rituals, the police are often unable to locate either the victim or the perpetrators. Suspects, arrested under suspicion of satanic activity, often respond rather strangely. When arrested, one vagrant carried a human bone in a pouch. Upon questioning he delivered a most shocking statement: "I have a problem. I am a cannibal!" However, nothing could be proven.

The Sociology of Satanic Cults

Dr. Edward J. Moody studied satanic cults in California from 1965 to 1969. He heard rumors of an Allhallows Eve (Halloween) celebration in a haunted house in San Francisco. His conclusions are worth noting. "Those who eventually become Satanists are attempting to cope with the everyday problems of life, with the here and now, rather than with some transcendental afterlife" ("Urban Witches," in *Conformity and Conflict: Readings in Cultural Anthropology,* eds. James P. Spradley and David W. McCurdy [New York: Little, Brown and Company, 1971], p. 288; quoted in Edward A. Tireyakian, ed., *On the Margin of the Visible: Sociology, the Esoteric and the Occult* [New York: John Wiley and Sons, 1974]).

As pressures increase, people choose many ways to cope with life. Many seek answers from supernatural sources. Curiously, some shun God but seek Satan. They want and get immediate answers as well as the satisfaction of some physical desire. Compare this with what Paul said long ago: "For although they knew God, they neither glorified Him as God nor gave thanks to Him, but their thinking became futile and their foolish hearts were darkened" (Romans 1:21). The results of shutting out God are not pleasant. Three times Paul reminds us that God "gave them over" to the desires of their flesh (Romans 1:24, 26, 28). As enemies of God, they will be "thrown into the lake of fire" (Revelation 20:15).

A Modern Satanic Grotto

Local satanic groups are called "grottoes." Their rituals and ceremonies are little more than a mockery of Christ. Following is a sample of what a typical ritual might include, as suggested by Moody's article.

> Every Friday evening just before midnight, a group of men and women gathers at a home in San Francisco; and there, under the guidance of their high priest, a sorcerer or magus sometimes called the "Black Pope of Satanism," they study and practice the ancient art of black magic. Precisely at midnight they perform satanic rituals that apparently differ little from those allegedly performed by European Satanists and witches at least as early as the seventh century. By the dim and flickering light of black candles, hooded figures perform their rites upon the traditional satanic altar—the naked body of a beautiful young witch—calling forth the mysterious powers of darkness to do their bidding. Beneath the emblem of Baphomet, the horned god, they engage in indulgences of flesh and sense for whose performance their forbearers suffered death and torture at the hands of earlier Christian zealots (*Conformity and Conflict*, p. 280).

All Satanists are not witches or wizards, but most dabble in black magic. Their activities are a blend of study and worship. The rituals give them the *feeling* of worship. Their altar, often a naked woman, is symbolic of a primary goal: to satisfy any physical desire.

Moody began as an observer but was drawn in as a willing participant. He was impressed by their sincerity. "They firmly believed in what they were doing!" At the same time, they wanted their activities to remain secret in order to prevent ridicule, censure, and even prosecution. They felt isolated by their bizarre behavior, but they continued anyway, since Satanism provided a sense of identity and seemed to provide answers to their problems.

Some satanic cults bear mysterious names such as "Brotherhood of the White Temple, Inc.," "Monastery of the Seven Rays," and "The Radiant School." Satanic cults make vague promises of personal wealth and success. Most recruits endure an initiation ceremony, pay an initiation fee, and experience some harmless magick. This smoke screen disguises the real evil—until recruits are hooked!

The Process

"The Process Church of the Final Judgment," also known simply as the Process, was founded in London, England, in 1963. The founders, a married couple named Moore who later changed their name to DeGrimston, were two ranking members of another cult, the Church of Scientology. The DeGrimstons actively recruited persons who had money and powerful positions. The cult originally held to two gods, Lucifer and Jehovah, but later added a third, Satan. The Process taught that by love, Christ and Satan would destroy their enmity and come together. After all, Christ had said "Love your enemy," and His enemy was Satan.

DeGrimston wrote, "If a man asks: What is the Process? Say to him: It is the End, the final ending of the world of men. It is the agent of The End, the instrument of The End, and the inexorable Power of the End" (quoted in Carl A. Raschke, *Painted Black* [New York: Harper & Row, 1990], p. 112).

On the surface, the words might sound somewhat harmless, even if strange. But to the Process, those words included the idea that its members could and should hasten the spiritual coming together of pure love from heaven with pure evil from hell. Therefore, followers of the Process believed that through murder, butchery, and flagrant use of sexuality, they could hastened the end. Hence the name "The Process Church of the Final Judgment." The group splintered in 1974 and spawned other groups.

In his book *The Ultimate Evil,* investigative reporter Maurey Terry pulled together some startling information. According to Terry, a well-organized network of satanic cults crisscrosses the U.S. As a result of extensive research, Terry concluded that both Charles Manson in California and the famous David Berkowitz/Son of Sam murderer in New York belonged to the same nationwide network of satanic cults related to the Process.

On the west coast, when Charles Manson left the Process church, his "family" consisted of Charlie (or Christ, as he was often called) and a dozen young ladies who alternately worshiped and slept with him. They were convicted of nine murders that occurred on April 9 and 10, 1969. Manson claimed that he had been sent to earth to create "helter skelter," which would hasten judgment and therefore Christ's return. While in jail awaiting trial, Manson spoke freely with police and reporters until he was visited by several members of the Process. After their visit Manson was strangely silent.

A dozen years later, David Berkowitz, also known as "Son of Sam," was convicted of the murder of a dozen people in New York City. (He claimed that a dog had ordered the killings. The dog was owned by someone named Sam, hence the nickname "Son of Sam.") Berkowitz taunted the police with notes to them and other public figures. He signed his name with an unusual and recognizable geometrical pattern. The murders were strangely focused around certain dates later proven to be significant to Satanists. One such date was Halloween, October 31. Another, April 30, known from the Middle Ages as Walpurgisnacht, had for centuries been celebrated as "Witch's Night." After his arrest, Berkowitz admitted that he was part of a satanic group of more than 20 members and had close connections to the Process.

Voodoo Cults?

The thought of voodoo conjures up thoughts of the deepest jungles of Africa or South America. A San Francisco police officer, Sandi Gallant, attracted national attention when she brought her knowledge of satanic crime to bear on a murder investigation. In 1981, she was notified of an unusual homicide in San Francisco's Golden Gate Park. The victim couldn't be easily identified, since the head was missing. There were several other unusual pieces of evidence, including a chicken's head left in place of the human head. As a result of her study, she suggested that the crime was a voodoo ritual known as Santeria. She predicted what would happen in the following 42 days. " 'They really thought we were nuts,' she says. 'Nobody believed it—until the investigator got a call in the middle of the night of the forty-second day.' " Someone had attempted to reunite the head with the body, which was still awaiting identification in the county morgue.

Although that case remains unsolved, the truth of her prediction gave her nationwide credibility as an expert on satanic crime (*San Francisco* magazine, August 1987, p. 82).

Why Satanism?

People become involved in Satanism in an attempt to cope with the problems of life. They may be frustrated because of real or imagined problems over which they seem to have no control. They may be chafing under a morality they believe to be too strict. They may have been physically or emotionally hurt by someone. Whatever the specific, everyone looks for help of some sort.

Christ invited, "Come to Me, all you who are weary and burdened, and I will give you rest. Take My yoke upon you and learn from Me, for I am gentle and humble in heart, and you will find rest for your souls. For My yoke is easy and My burden is light" (Matthew 11:28–30). Sometimes, though, we humans can't feel the load being made lighter. Jesus' promise may not even seem true when looking at the suffering in the world. So, many people want a quicker, easier fix to problems—the very solution Satan seems to offer.

Recall the attractions that Satan dangled before Jesus: bread, power, and position (Matthew 4:1–11). Fortunately for us, Christ saw through Satan's thinly disguised promises. He successfully resisted Satan's temptations. With Christ's Word in our heart and on our lips, we too can resist Satan, and he will—must—flee from us (James 4:7). Be clear about why Christ came to earth. "The reason the Son of God appeared was to destroy the devil's work" (1 John 3:8). "And having disarmed the powers and authorities, He made a public spectacle of them, triumphing over them by the cross" (Colossians 2:15).

Satan's greatest tool is fear, but in Jesus we have nothing to fear. In his hymn "A Mighty Fortress Is Our God,"

Martin Luther wrote, "We tremble not, we fear no ill, They shall not overpow'r us. This world's prince may still Scowl fierce as he will, He can harm us none, He's judged; the deed is done; One little word can fell him" (*Lutheran Worship* 298).

One little word! That one little word is the name of Jesus. Although the thought of satanic cults can frighten us, never take your eyes off Jesus and His cross. He purchased forgiveness and paid for your eternal life. So live for Him!

6

Do-It-Yourself Satanism

While investigating a suspected arson in 1986, a fire marshall discovered what he thought was a simple star-shaped decoration. Also found at the scene was the decapitated, mutilated body of a cat. Investigators connected the fire to a teenage gang in the area. The mother of a gang member identified the star as five-pointed pentagram, which her son and his friends often displayed upside down to identify music they enjoyed. The walls in his room were covered with similar symbols. The boy, who had been performing ritual sacrifices, and his friends were self-styled Satanists. They had learned about Aleister Crowley and Anton LaVey and had read *The Satanic Bible*. They were simply copying the bizarre things they had read about.

Self-styled Satanists differ from those mentioned in the previous two chapters. They are unstructured, and they behave in far more bizarre ways than the more organized and visible satanic groups. Some go so far to gain a supernatural "power high" that they take a human life—their own or someone else's.

Self-styled Satanists are probably more visible, since people are more likely to know about their activities. Few people would attend a satanic church, but many might stumble upon a group of self-styled Satanists and become intrigued by their strange behavior. Such initiation could lead to deeper involvement. Many dismiss reports of self-styled Satanists as innocent teenage behavior gone awry.

But other age groups are also vulnerable.

All three types of Satanists ("churches," cults, and self-styled) have a common thread: they worship and serve Satan. Most get involved through an innocent contact. They are later enticed to continue involvement through the use of drugs and sex. But the hook is set when new recruits are allowed to observe and actually participate in a satanic ritual, which is often an adaptation or portion of the Black Mass.

Where Do They Get Their Information?

The *20/20* news presentation referred to in chapter 5 suggested that self-styled Satanists learn about Satanism in three major ways: through literature, music, and movies. The program's reporter stood in a shopping mall in front of three stores, each offering one of the three sources. Of the three, however, music with satanic overtones seemed to have the greatest influence, especially on young people.

The lives and music of rock musicians, particularly the heavy metal variety, suggest that rebellion and complete lawlessness are attractive. The lyrics of such music, often coupled with visual effects, promote sinful behavior and every imaginable evil desire. Within the past 10 years, 24-hour rock music cable television stations have filled the air waves with violence and encouragement of rebellious behavior.

Many books and articles have been written warning youth and their parents of the potential danger. Several are *Why Knock Rock,* by Dan and Steve Peters (Minneapolis: Bethany, 1984); *Larson's Book of Rock,* by Bob Larson (Wheaton: Tyndale, 1987); and *Raising PG Kids in an X-Rated Society,* by Tipper Gore (Nashville: Abingdon, 1987).

One young man researched and wrote a paper on

another religion. He had chosen the Hindu religion, but in the course of his research he became interested in another topic he had stumbled upon: Satanism. He buried himself in books about the topic. Within weeks, he became hostile. He became obsessed with heavy metal music with strong satanic influences. His teachers noticed a change and called it to the attention of his mother. His father noted that the boy had quickly turned from model airplanes to the occult. He could be heard singing lyrics about blood and killing one's mother. Soon both the boy and his mother were dead—by the boy's own hand. Investigators found that he had planned the murder-suicide after endlessly listening to several heavy metal rock songs. His friends said that he felt this was the only way out of a difficult childhood.

Some rock music is little more than a thinly disguised directive for destruction. Attempts at rating music have been met with mixed reactions. Some artists resent it. Others favor it, believing it will encourage their audiences to buy more! With computers we say, "Garbage in, garbage out." What shall we say when garbage is shoved into the minds of impressionable young people? Sadly, such lyrics are perfectly legal. That is why it is so important for parents to listen to music *with* their teens. The apostle Paul wrote, "Finally, brothers, whatever is true, whatever is noble, whatever is right, whatever is pure, whatever is lovely, whatever is admirable—if anything is excellent or praiseworthy—think about such things" (Philippians 4:8).

The freedom to produce satanic literature is guaranteed by the first amendment to our U.S. Constitution. Satan clearly uses that freedom. The most common source of satanic literature is the public library or corner bookstore. Librarians admit that satanic literature is popular. And after a book has been checked out, it is often "lost" or never returned.

One youth described his initiation into Satanism. He

and a friend were browsing through a bookstore. His friend accidentally bumped a shelf and a book fell out. The first boy was intrigued by the cover's strange-looking photograph of author Anton LaVey. The book was *The Satanic Bible*. Out of curiosity, the boy bought and read the book.

Then he acted out what he read. Following his arrest for the murder of a 12-year-old girl, he said almost proudly, "I am a Satanist!" He is now serving a life prison sentence. His father admitted that although *The Satanic Bible* sounded innocent, if taken literally, it was really quite dangerous.

How close can you get without being burned? Being tempted into Satanism is almost a compliment from your enemy! The closer you get to God, the harder Satan works. Many books available in libraries and bookstores not only talk about Satanism, they initiate the reader into it. It is quite legal and highly intriguing.

The Satanic Bible and its companion volume, *The Satanic Rituals*, may sound innocent. After all, the concepts proposed in LaVey's nine statements (See Chapter 4) don't seem very different from the lifestyle glorified by most movies and TV shows. But indulgence in any and all pleasure is very dangerous. Satan is fishing for God's people. His sharp, barbed hook is baited. By the time some realize what Satanism really is, it is too late. Satan has already set the hook.

Movies/Videos

In 1988 several newspaper headlines rocked the nation. "Rochester, Minnesota youth charged in quadruple slaying." A month later the same newspapers reported, "Four teens charged in vampire-style killing." These stories were connected by satanic and ritualistic overtones.

The boy in the first story listened to heavy metal, anarchist, punk rock groups. He also frequently argued with his parents about the clothes he wore and the music videos he listened to. On the plus side, he was an athlete, a hard worker, and definitely not a psycho. The night before the murders, the boy had told a friend that he planned to kill his parents. He did—plus two other family members. Rock music was his influence.

The second crime ruined five families. During a camping trip along the Mississippi, four teens had killed a friend. When arrested, one suspect admitted drinking the blood of the victim. Vampirism had often been a topic of discussion among the boys. Their talks had intensified after viewing a rented movie, *Lost Boys,* a story about teenage vampires.

Several interesting things happened as a result of this crime. The manager of the video store that had rented the movie immediately pulled his copies off the shelves. (However, he did not remove other movies with similar occult and satanic suggestions.) Then the manager of another video store phoned, asking to purchase all his copies because *Lost Boys* was among the most popular titles. Everyone, it seemed, wanted to see the movie in spite of its inherent evil.

Is it really possible for movies to influence people to do such unthinkable things? How much influence does a movie actually have on a person? Are these influences stronger on teens? Should movies, music, and other media be censored? Who's to decide? Movies like *The Exorcist* and *Rosemary's Baby* paved the way for many others. Thousands of people came to see these movies out of curiosity and left in either horror or fear. Some, however, only

L evels or kinds of satanic involvement indicate Satanism's progressive nature. (1) **Fun and games**; (2) **the dabblers**; (3) **criminal activity**; and (4) **organized Satanists**.

whet their curiosity and appetites for more. In the same *20/20* broadcast mentioned earlier, former satanic high-priest-turned-Christian-evangelist Mike Warnke said, "If the devil has PR, then it is cinema."

Browse the shelves of a local video rental store. The *Friday the Thirteenth* movie series and *Texas Chainsaw Massacre* contain strong suggestions of Satanism. Opening scenes in the movie *Ghoulies* depict an actual satanic Black Mass. The *Omen* movie series encourages young people to dabble in the occult. The implications are clear. People want the same powers that characters in the movies have. The satanic ideas in some of these movies are subtle, but often they are obvious and always dangerous. The credits at the end of a movie are seldom studied carefully. But those at the end of *Rosemary's Baby* include the name of the technical director, Anton LaVey!

Satanic temptation also travels down the seemingly harmless path paved with games and toys. Consider the supernatural powers demonstrated by Saturday morning cartoon characters. Sure, they're make-believe. But what subtle messages about the supernatural are children picking up? Each family must make individual decisions about the diet of listening, viewing, and playing they consume. "You are what you eat" also applies to spiritual things.

In fantasy-role playing (FRP) games such as Dungeons and Dragons, players actually assume the personalities of their characters. As play progresses, players cast spells including "death curses." After her son committed suicide as a direct result of his involvement with FRP games, Pat Pulling founded an organization called "Bothered about Dungeons and Dragons." The group has documented proof of numerous teen suicides closely related to Dungeons and Dragons and other FRP games. They are not games any longer.

What's a Christian to Do?

Satan is cunning. He works hard to trick God's people. Many people may want to throw up their hands in despair and say, "What's a Christian to do? Is there anything a Christian can read, see, or think about that isn't somehow satanic?"

In the story of the Trojan horse, rather than attack the city of Troy directly, Greek soldiers built a huge, hollow, wooden horse. They left it in front of the gates of the city of Troy. Thinking the horse a gift, the Trojans wheeled it inside the city walls to admire it. After the Trojans fell asleep, the Greeks crept out of their hiding place inside the horse and took the city by surprise.

Satan often operates like that—he attacks from behind, where he is least expected. This is why Peter warns us to be on guard. "Your enemy the devil prowls around like a roaring lion looking for someone to devour. Resist him, standing firm in the faith" (1 Peter 5:8–9).

7

Conclusion: From a Christian Perspective

It has been said several times: The devil is strong, dangerous, and real, but Christ is stronger. However, although the devil is a defeated enemy, he is not about to lie down and play dead (2 Thessalonians 2:9). Like a chicken with its head cut off, Satan is in his death throes. He tries to drag others down into hell with him. Satan was active in Jesus' day and is still active today.

We know how Jesus responded when Satan confronted Him. But how about modern Christians? Many people weren't taught about Jesus when they were young. Others have learned the truth about Christ's free gift of eternal life but have drifted away from His offer. Some choose Satan and evil over God and His good. When Satan rears his ugly head, how will you respond?

The apostle Paul knew that troubled times would come just before the end of the world. He encouraged his friends to "put on the armor of light" (Romans 13:12). Look to the power of the Holy Spirit to protect you. Avoid the sinful dark-

A word of warning. Even though you believe in Jesus, you may not recognize the presence of Satan and his evil tricks. You need to turn to God and His Word often. "Test everything" (1 Thessalonians 5:21). Be sure that your words and works are of God and that your faith is not threatened or compromised.

ness of the desires of your own heart. Always draw upon the strength of Christ. "Finally, be strong in the Lord and in His mighty power. Put on the full armor of God so that you can take your stand against the devil's schemes" (Ephesians 6:10–11). Your faith, like a suit of armor, will protect you. Each piece in the suit of armor is designed to protect.

The sword of the Spirit, the Word of God, however, is also used to attack. With the sword of the Spirit you have the power of Christ to battle against Satan. Examine the dangers of the occult and Satanism. Learn to recognize Satan's temptations. Stand firm with God's Word. Take a definite stand *against* Satan and *for* Christ. There is no room to sit on the fence. Christ said, "He who is not with Me is against Me, and he who does not gather with Me scatters" (Matthew 12:30).

The rapid increase of Satanism is a sign of the approaching judgment. Satan has devised clever schemes to turn God's people away from God. It is especially important for persons in authority to be aware of these temptations and to help others stand against them. Parents, teachers, and pastors take these warnings seriously, for as the end approaches the responsibility for directing people to Jesus and away from the devil becomes more important and more difficult.

Where Do You Stand?

Have you heard this question before: "(Name), do you renounce the devil and all his works and all his ways?" In Baptism you renounced Satan once. But you may also daily renounce him and recommit yourself to Christ. In his *Daily Renewal of Baptism,* Martin Luther suggested that, upon arising, each Christian make the sign of the cross and remember what happened in Baptism. Ask, "Have I opened any doors for Satan to enter even a tiny corner of my life? Are there lingering doubts which would allow Satan a foothold to confuse me?" Christians who have in any way dabbled with the occult or Satanism will humbly come before God and repent of their sin. Such resisting of the devil will cause him to flee.

Degrees of Involvement in Satanism

When wading into a cool lake in the spring, different people venture to a different depth, depending on their own comfort. Similarly, with Satanism people get involved to different degrees. The first level is satanic *influence.* As sinners, we hear and, at times, give in to the tempter's voice. Daily, therefore, we pray for and receive God's forgiveness. Satanic *obsession* is more intense and occurs when people surround themselves with satanic influences. They become curious about and then fascinated by the supernatural powers of Satan. But obsession can quickly lead to the next level, *domination.* Here, fascination with Satan and his evil takes priority in a person's life. The final degree of satanic involvement is *possession.* Although rare and difficult to diagnose, satanic possession occurs when the devil has literally taken over a person and controls him or her. Usually such persons exhibit the marks of the demoniac as described in Mark 5:2–7.

Persons in authority must be alert. Dabbling in the occult and Satanism can open the door for more intense and dangerous involvement. Teens and preteens are most vulnerable because of peer pressure. Some young people may do anything to be accepted. They discover too late that they

Many people, without intending to do great harm to themselves or others, have gotten involved in Satanism and are in over their heads. They have become involved in Satanism through drugs, alcohol, and/or promiscuous sex. These often lead into crimes of arson, vandalism, animal abuse, and even murder.

have entered a trap from which they feel they cannot escape. Of course, since Christ is stronger, they cannot go too far for Christ to rescue them.

Marks of Satanic Involvement

Although not conclusive, there are clues to satanic involvement that may signal a need for concern: dressing only in black; wearing an inverted cross, crucifix, pentagram, skull earrings, or other jewelry fashioned in pentagrams; displaying satanic pictures or symbols such as "666"; and puncture wounds either on oneself or on animals such as family pets. More conclusive signs include possession of a satanic altar, black candles, or a collection of bones. Many Satanists possess a *Book of Shadows*, a personal diary of involvement in satanic rituals. Satanists also carry Anton LaVey's *The Satanic Bible* or *The Satanic Rituals.*

Although less obvious and not limited to occult and satanic involvement, other signs are to be heeded. These may include drug abuse or sudden and unexplained mood swings, especially an intense rebelliousness. Many new Satanists suddenly have new friends, exhibit a change in performance at school or work, or have unexplained absences from home or work. They may either seek isolation or express a fear of being alone.

It is important to remember that people quickly and thoroughly become like the forces they admit into their lives, whether Christ or Satan. If you are dealing with someone you suspect has become involved with Satanism, remember there never has been a happy Satanist. Satan is the Father of lies. Those who seek happiness and contentment in Satanism find that it forever eludes them. Instead they are plagued by emptiness and a gnawing sense of failure.

Prevention Is Still the Best Medicine

Christians must take positive action against Satan. Here are some positive things a Christian can do.

1. *Realize that Satan is real,* even if invisible. As we have seen, St. Paul reminds us in Ephesians 6:12 that our struggle is against real spiritual forces of evil. The devil is as personal a being as God is. Don't be content just to take a private stand; warn others.

2. *Be alert to Satan's motives and methods,* the ways he prowls around seeking to devour people spiritually. Study the Scriptures in order to understand the ways Satan attacked Adam and Eve (Genesis 3:1–5), Job (Job 1–2), or Christ Himself (Matthew 4:1–11). Because Satan attacks our weaknesses, note them—including any false confidence in your spirituality. "If you think you are standing firm, be careful that you don't fall" (1 Corinthians 10:12). Test every spirit that comes to you (1 John 4:1). Satan is a master of clever disguises, even appearing like an angel of light (2 Corinthians 11:14). Since you probably wouldn't be fooled by a talking serpent, Satan won't try that one on you. However, in an attempt to keep Jesus from going to the cross, the devil was so bold as to speak through the words of one of Jesus' own disciples (Matthew 16:22–23). Anything that stands in the way of telling others about Christ's death and resurrection is satanic. *Be aware* and *beware!*

3. *"Resist the devil"* (James 4:7). Be ready to resist Satan however and whenever he tries to lead you away from Christ. Resist Satan by boldly making a clear testimony of your faith in a Savior who died and rose for your sins. Cultivate the fruit of the Spirit (Galatians 5:22–23) as God feeds and nourishes you through Word and sacrament.

4. *Cling to the cross of Christ.* Never forget what Christ did for you. Although not scriptural, the Hollywood idea of warding off vampires with a cross illustrates Satan's weakness and the power of our Lord. By ourselves we are no match for Satan. But when we cling to Christ's cross—with the message of Christ's death and resurrection—Satan must run from us. "They overcame him by the blood of the Lamb and by the word of their testimony" (Revelation 12:11).

In his book *The Renewed Mind,* Larry Christenson tells a story called "The Old Landlord." Suppose you live in an apartment with a landlord who makes life miserable. He demands high rent. When you can't pay, he agrees to loan you the money but at an extremely high rate of interest. He also barges into your apartment at anytime and messes up the place. He then charges you damages because you aren't keeping things up. Your life is miserable. One day there is a gentle knock at your door. The caller identifies Himself as your new landlord. He has purchased the building, will remodel it, and lower your rent. How do you feel? Great! But soon the old landlord knocks again and demands his rent. Will you pay or try to fight him by yourself?

Let us fix our eyes on Jesus, the author and perfecter of our faith, who for the joy set before Him endured the cross, scorning its shame, and sat down at the right hand of the throne of God. Consider Him who endured such opposition from sinful men, so that you will not grow weary and lose heart" (Hebrews 12:2–3).

This is exactly how it is for Christians. We have been bought and paid for by the blood of Jesus Christ (1 Corinthians 6:20; 1 Peter 1:18–19). Yet when Satan comes to make further claims on our lives, we think that we must give in to him. We must tell Satan to take up the matter with our new landlord, Jesus Christ. No matter how many times Satan returns, even with the same temptation, we must send him to Jesus.

Responding to Satanism in Society

God has placed His people in the world, but they are not of the world. Christians speak a powerful witness to others when they support all that is noble and uplifting. Christians who are aware of the dangers of the occult and Satanism should refuse to patronize and support movies, videos, and books that compromise the standards of morality and life that God loves. When Christians find an open door for a witness for Christ, they need to confidently and boldly step through it. "In your hearts set apart Christ as Lord. Always be prepared to give an answer to everyone who asks you to give the reason for the hope that you have" (1 Peter 3:15).

Once, when Jesus' followers returned from sharing the Good News with people Jesus said, "I saw Satan fall like lightning from heaven" (Luke 10:18). It was almost as if Satan were trying to climb back up to heaven again. Each time one of God's people shares the message of God's love and forgiveness, Satan falls back down again. Whenever Christ's love is lifted up, Satan is pushed down. Because Christ lives in us, we can lift Him up in any situation. Jesus, who lives in us, is greater than Satan who is in the world (1 John 4:4). Jesus holds us tightly and will never let us go (John 10:28).

> In all these things we are more than conquerors through Him who loved us. For I am convinced that neither death nor life, neither angels nor demons, neither the present nor the future, nor any powers, neither height nor depth, nor anything else in all creation, will be able to separate us from the love of God that is in Christ Jesus our Lord. (Romans 8:37–39)

Resources

DeHann, Richard W. *Satan, Satanism, and Witchcraft.* Grand Rapids, MI: Zondervan, 1972.

Hoover, David. *How to Respond to the Occult.* St. Louis: Concordia Publishing House, 1977.

Lochhass, Philip. *The New Age Movement.* Rev. ed. How to Respond series. St. Louis: Concordia Publishing House, 1995.

Michaelson, Johanna. *The Beautiful Side of Evil.* Eugene, OR: Harvest House, 1982.

Phillips, Phil. *Turmoil in the Toybox.* Lancaster, PA: Starburst, 1986.

Raschke, Carl A. *Painted Black.* New York: Harper & Row, 1990.